A
Literature Unit
for

The Adventures of Huckleberry Finn

by Mark Twain

Written by

Michael H. Levin, M.A.

Teacher Created Materials, Inc.
P.O. Box 1040
Huntington Beach, CA 92647
©1996 Teacher Created Materials, Inc.
Made in U.S.A.

ISBN 1-55734-564-3

Illustrated by
Ken Tunell

Edited by
Walter Kelly, M.A.

Cover Art by
Agi Palinay

Table Of Contents

Introduction

A good book can touch our lives like a good friend. Within its pages are words and characters that can inspire us to achieve our highest ideals. We can turn to it for companionship, recreation, comfort, and guidance. It can also give us a cherished story to hold in our hearts forever.

In *Literature Units*, great care has been taken to select books that are sure to become good friends!

Teachers who use this unit will find the following features to supplement their own valuable ideas.

- Sample lesson plans
- Pre-reading activities
- Notes to the teacher
- A biographical sketch and picture of the author
- A book summary
- Vocabulary lists and suggested vocabulary activities

- Chapters grouped for study with each section including:

  - *quizzes*
  - *hands-on projects*
  - *cooperative learning activities*
  - *cross-curriculum connections*
  - *extensions into the reader's own life*

- Post-reading activities
- Book report ideas
- Research activity
- Culminating activities
- Three different options for unit tests
- Bibliography of related reading
- Answer key

We are confident this unit will be a valuable addition to your planning, and we hope your students will increase the circle of "friends" they have in books as you use these ideas!

Sample Lesson Plan

Each of the lessons suggested below can take from one to several days to complete.

Lesson 1
- Introduce and complete some or all of the pre-reading activities found on page 5.
- Tap into your students' understanding. (page 6)
- Rank problems that can hurt a growing child. (page 7)
- Work with multiple intelligences. (page 8)
- Read "About the Author" with your students. (page 10)
- Introduce the vocabulary list for Section 1. (page 12)

Lesson 2
- Read Chapters I through XI. As you read, place the vocabulary words in the context of the story and discuss their meanings.
- Do a vocabulary activity. (page 13)
- Make a quilt piece. (page 15)
- Discover dialect. (page 16)
- Begin "Reading Response Journals." (page 17)
- Tickle your funny bone. (page 18)
- Administer Section 1 quiz. (page 14)
- Introduce the vocabulary list for Section 2. (page 12)

Lesson 3
- Read Chapters XII through XXIII. Place the vocabulary words in context and discuss their meanings.
- Do a vocabulary activity. (page 13)
- Write and record your own version of how the novel ends. (page 20)
- Discuss how you would like living on the raft. (page 21)
- Draw the raft on the river from Huck's description. (page 22)
- Use life experiences to consider living on your own. (page 23)
- Administer Section 2 quiz. (page 19)
- Introduce the vocabulary list for Section 3. (page 12)

Lesson 4
- Read Chapters XXIV through XXXI. Place the vocabulary words in context and discuss their meanings.
- Do a vocabulary activity. (page 13)
- Cook some old-fashioned candies. (page 25)
- Decide what is truth and what is lying. (page 26)
- Learn about the Mississippi River. (page 27)
- Find out about making important choices. (page 28)
- Administer Section 3 quiz. (page 24)
- Introduce the vocabulary list for Section 4. (page 12)

Lesson 5
- Read Chapters XXXII through XLIII. Place the vocabulary words in context and discuss their meanings.
- Do a vocabulary activity. (page 13)
- Make a travel brochure. (page 30)
- Create adult confusion. (page 31)
- Learn songs of the period. (page 32)
- Examine what you do well. (page 33)
- Administer Section 4 quiz. (page 29)

Lesson 6
- Examine Huck's life experiences. (page 34)
- Discuss any questions your students have about the story. (page 35)
- Assign book report and research activity. (pages 36 and 37)
- Begin work on one or more culminating activities. (pages 38 and 41)

Lesson 7
- Administer Unit Tests: 1, 2, and/or 3. (pages 42, 43, and 44)
- Discuss the test answers and possibilities.
- Discuss the students' enjoyment of the book.
- Provide a list of related reading for your students. (page 45)

Before the Book

Before you begin reading *The Adventures of Huckleberry Finn* with your students, do some pre-reading activities to stimulate interest and enhance comprehension. Here are some activities that might work for your class.

1. What have you heard about this novel? What information do you already know?

2. Predict what the story might be about just by looking at the cover illustration.

3. Discuss other books by Mark Twain that students may have heard about or read.

4. Respond to the following:

   ❑ Are you interested in . . .

   - stories about children who have to be heroic?
   - stories with adventure and life-or-death struggles?
   - stories dealing with a young person having experiences that make him/her grow up?
   - stories that show a young person is capable of making important decisions and taking action?
   - stories that have both funny and sad incidents?

   ❑ Why might young boys or girls be forced to live on their own without anyone taking care of them?

   ❑ How can unusual occurrences change a young person's life?

   ❑ What is it like being in a new and completely different environment?

5. Work in groups to create a factual and/or fictional story about a boy who leaves his home and has strange adventures.

6. Write descriptions or brainstorm ideas about what makes a person strong or courageous.

7. Use the picture on page 48 to introduce *The Adventures of Huckleberry Finn* to your class. The picture can also be used as a journal cover for Reading Response Journals (page 17) or as the centerpiece of a bulletin board display of student work. After the novel has been completed, the picture may be used to stimulate discussion about the symbolism of the two figures as they journey together down the great river.

Tapping into Your Understanding

You have many years of experience which have made you the person you are today. An author expects you to bring that experience to the novel he or she has written. In order for you to get the most out of your reading of *Huckleberry Finn*, consider the statements below. (Although they relate to situations in the novel, each should be considered from the viewpoint of your own life. After you finish *Huck Finn*, you can discuss how Mark Twain views each statement and whether it is similar to your own understanding.)

Your teacher might want to have an oral discussion before you write your answers.

1. It is acceptable to lie to protect a friend who is in trouble.

   _____

   _____

   _____

2. It is acceptable to break the law in some situations.

   _____

   _____

   _____

3. It is acceptable to pretend you are someone you are not when meeting a stranger.

   _____

   _____

   _____

4. Adults will usually try to take advantage of children.

   _____

   _____

   _____

5. Honor is more important than truth.

   _____

   _____

   _____

6. Females are kinder and more honest than males.

   _____

   _____

   _____

7. Your first impression of someone is usually the right one.

   _____

   _____

   _____

Rankings

Directions: The following are problems a young person might face in growing up. These are also some of the problems Huck faces in the novel. Rank them from one to ten, according to how damaging they might be.

1—least damaging

10—most damaging

———————— feeling you are not very smart

———————— living with one parent only

———————— being forced to leave home and live on your own

———————— having no brothers or sisters

———————— finding no help or comfort from religion

———————— constantly being told that your feelings and ideas are not any good

———————— meeting people who want to take advantage of you

———————— not being allowed to go to school

———————— living with a physically and mentally abusive parent

———————— being considered by members of your town as not as good (worthy) as they are

- Discuss your choices with another member of your class. Were your choices the same? How did they differ?

- Discuss answers with your teacher. How many of the class picked the same item for number 1? How many picked the same item for number 10? Why do you think the choices differed? Could it have to do with a person's own life experiences? How?

Multiple Intelligences

Howard Gardner's theory of multiple intelligences is well known but is often difficult to incorporate into our lesson plans. Most of us would probably agree that Huck Finn had the ability to learn in many different categories. (Your students might want to consider which type of learner Huck was and support it with evidence from the novel.) Below is a review of Gardner's ideas as stated in *Frames of Mind*, 1985, along with a possible activity based on each for *Huck Finn*. It might make an appropriate extra-credit assignment for your class.

Type of Learning	Activity
Linguistic: sensitivity to the meaning of words, to the grammar of language; ability to use language to convince others, to use language to remember; prefers written directions to reading a map; thinks in words.	Assign these students to work on explaining the dialect in the novel, especially the dialogue spoken by Jim.
Logical-Mathematical: ability to manipulate numerical quantities, symbols, and operations; tends to be questioning and curious; likely to have solid rationales for decisions; looks for patterns, relationships.	Assign these students to report on what they feel is hard to understand or rationalize in the actions of the characters in the novel.
Spatial: ability to image; ability to rotate objects in the mind's eye; can read maps, graphs; learns visually; learns through art.	Assign this group to research art of the period and report to the class. Look for information on the landscape painters of the "Hudson River School" (Thomas Cole, Edwin Church, Albert Bierstadt, and George Inness).
Musical: sensitivity to music and sound; can learn through rhythm, rhyme, and pattern.	Assign students to research music of mid-nineteenth century. Stephen Foster would be the most important composer.
Bodily-Kinesthetic: ability to use one's body skillfully and expressively with great control; can learn through drama, movement, and touch.	Have these students dramatize a scene from the novel.
Intrapersonal: ability to examine one's own feelings; intuitive; works best on one's own in privacy; self-motivating.	These students can help the class to understand Huck's motivation in the novel. They may want to work alone—give each a different section.
Interpersonal: ability to read the intentions, motivations, and temperaments of others; empathetic to others; charismatic leader; counselor, teacher; learns best through interaction, cooperation.	As a group, these students will help the class to understand the changing relationship of Huck and Jim.

Notes to the Teacher

Teaching *Huckleberry Finn* can be a wonderful experience for you and your students. It is a book that captures so much of the American spirit as well as allowing you to discuss some of America's problems. Since it is a book that has been banned by some school districts on racial, religious, and societal grounds, you should clearly consider these concerns before beginning the novel.

Mark Twain believed that in a battle between nature and society, nature was clearly the winner. Huck survives in spite of what he has learned from society. By going against school and church teachings, Huck feels he is wrong but goes with his "natural" feelings anyway. His natural feelings are generally correct. They are absolutely correct when it comes to his ultimate treatment of Jim. Remember—in the pre-Civil War South, both the school and church taught that slavery was decent and necessary.

You may need to discuss how society's teachings could be wrong in the past and how such teachings change. Or perhaps you might feel that what school and church taught in 1850 in Missouri was a corruption of what they should have been teaching. As teachers, we certainly believe in the importance of education. Perhaps we might want to say that although we appreciate that Twain felt education and society were poor substitutes for "natural" understanding, beliefs can change. It might be an excellent time to introduce the concept of understanding what a writer is saying, while not agreeing with his or her philosophies.

We must also be concerned with the term "nigger" which is used so often in the novel. It must be dealt with directly. In 1845, this term was not considered racist by the vast majority of citizens in Missouri. It is the only term Huck knew to call black people. The terms "black" and "African American" were not in use. The acceptable "Negro" was not used with any regularity in the South at this time. Notice that Jim also used the term "nigger" in the novel when referring to himself.

When having the students write about the novel, you might wish to substitute "Negro" at all times. You must decide whether it is acceptable to use "nigger" in a direct quote. Please be concerned, especially, with black children in your classroom. No matter what you say, the term "nigger" will probably hurt them every time they see it in print. Reinforcing that it was the acceptable term may allow them to endure it on an intellectual level but might not on an emotional one.

One last note: *Huck Finn* is a perfect vehicle with which to teach irony. Young readers, however, may have a problem sorting it out when it comes to Huck struggling with his conscience about whether to "turn Jim in." It must be reinforced that Huck does not understand the dramatic irony that is clear to the reader. Huck truly believes he is morally wrong by not returning a slave to his owner. (Huck rarely sees irony in the episodes during his journey. However street-wise he may be, intellectually he is naive.) He honestly thinks he will "go to hell" for helping Jim to freedom. Make sure your students understand that they can know the irony in a situation while the character involved does not.

About the Author

At the beginning of the 20th century, Mark Twain was probably the most instantly recognized person in the United States. His wild white hair, bushy eyebrows and mustache, and white linen suit were world famous. He was certainly the most successful American author of his day, and his lecture tours, as well as his books, made him a rich man.

Twain began life as Samuel Langhorne Clemens in Florida, Missouri, in 1835. He began having articles published in *The Saturday Evening Post* magazine when he was only 15. These were nonfiction pieces about Hannibal, Missouri, where he had lived most of his boyhood. Hannibal served as the setting for his famous novel *The Adventures of Tom Sawyer,* as well as the first part of *The Adventures of Huckleberry Finn*, where Twain renamed the town St. Petersburg.

Twain's first literary success was a short story, "The Celebrated Jumping Frog of Calaveras County," which concerned a contest of how far frogs could jump. It takes place in the gold country of California where Twain had traveled after being in the Civil War. Earlier Twain had trained to become a riverboat pilot on the Mississippi River, but when the Civil War began in 1861, he had to leave the river to become a Confederate soldier. Not believing in the practice of slavery, Twain left the army for the West.

By this time Samuel Clemens was using the name most people know him by, Mark Twain, which comes from a term used on the Mississippi River to call out the safe navigation depth for a steamboat. Twain became a newspaper reporter on the Nevada *Territorial Enterprise* after he had failed as a miner. Soon after his success with "The Jumping Frog" Twain saw his talents as a writer of fiction and published his first novel, *Innocents Abroad*, about Americans traveling in Europe in 1869.

Twain married Olivia Langdon in 1870 and had three daughters—Suzy, Clara, and Jane, and a son, Langdon. Besides *Tom Sawyer* and *Huckleberry Finn*, Twain's most popular novels continue to be *The Prince and the Pauper, Life on the Mississippi*, and *A Connecticut Yankee in King Arthur's Court.*

Despite business failures and the great sadness caused by the deaths of his wife and three of his children, Twain continued to write and lecture throughout his later life. Today he is still considered the foremost humorist America has produced, and his works are probably known by more Americans than those of any other writer.

The Adventures of Huckleberry Finn

by Mark Twain

(Bantam, 1985)
(available in Canada and UK, Doubleday Dell Seal; AUS, Transworld Publishers)

The Adventures of Huckleberry Finn is considered the finest book written by Mark Twain. Ernest Hemingway, the 20th century American who won the Nobel Prize for Literature, said "All modern American literature comes from one book by Mark Twain called *Huckleberry Finn.*" That is great praise for a book which seems a simple story of how a young boy learns about life in the pre-Civil War South. Huck, who is approximately 12 years of age, narrates his journey down the Mississippi River accompanied by the runaway slave, Jim.

Huckleberry Finn is an outcast from the white society of St. Petersburg (Hannibal), Missouri. The character, introduced in Twain's *The Adventures of Tom Sawyer*, has become wealthy by finding a robber's treasure in the earlier novel. He currently lives with the Widow Douglas and her sister, Miss Watson. Although he is not badly treated, he yearns for the freedom he had before having to go to school and become "regular and decent." His friends are Tom Sawyer and his "gang."

Huck's father, Pap, a cruel alcoholic, returns to St. Petersburg when he hears Huck is wealthy. He steals the boy and locks him up in the woods on the Illinois shore across the Mississippi River from St. Petersburg. Huck escapes by simulating his own death and goes to live on Jackson's Island in the middle of the river. There he finds Jim, Miss Watson's slave. Jim has run away from his owner when he finds out she is going to sell him down the river to New Orleans.

The central part of the novel concerns Huck and Jim's journey down the Mississippi River into Arkansas. Huck learns to respect Jim's friendship through a number of episodes. Huck realizes Jim is as "human" as he is. Jim treats Huck in much the way a real father would act toward his son. Huck also finds that Jim's concern for his daughter is the same as that of any caring "white" person.

Huck also learns about human nature when he is involved in the Grangerford-Shepherdson feud and witnesses the mob rule of the Boggs-Colonel Sherburn episode. Huck soon realizes that he has more freedom on the raft away from society. Society has rules that do not appeal to Huck. On the raft he is free to live by his own resources. When society, in the form of the king and the duke, appears on the raft, freedom is again taken away from Huck and Jim.

Jim is sold into slavery by the king. Huck makes up his mind to "steal" Jim back. Even though this is against everything Huck has learned is honest in the pre-Civil War South, he makes up his mind to reclaim his friend. Tom Sawyer re-enters the novel at this point, and the two plan how to free Jim. When Jim is bravely willing to give up his freedom to save a wounded Tom, the novel comes to an end —but not before Huck lays his plans to sneak away so he does not have to return to St. Petersburg where society will try to again "sivilize" him.

Vocabulary Lists

On this page are vocabulary lists which correspond to each sectional grouping of chapters. Vocabulary activity ideas can be found on page 13 of this book. On the left are conventional words. On the right are examples of slang found in the novel. Also included is some of the river vocabulary you may want your students to know.

Standard Terms

Section 1
(Chapters I–XI)

dismal	rushes
fidgety	whetstone
highwayman	carcass
counterfeit	hail (v.)
slouch hat	abreast
shanty	tolerable
roust	reticule

Section 2
(Chapters XII–XXIII)

dauphin (dolphin)	carpet-bag
solemn	temperance
pensive	tar and feather
disposition	phrenology
obiturary	encore
tribute	coax
aristocracy	lynch
ornery	

Section 3
(Chapters XIV–XXXI)

rapscallion	candid
frauds	sluice
pious	ingenious
passel	cravat
impostor	venture
pallet	bearings
notion	bogus

Section 4
(Chapters XXXII–XLIII)

waylay	desperadoes
impudent	rummage
scornful	sultry
insurrection	brash
fidget	

Slang Terms

Section 1
(Chapters I–XI)

hogshead	sass
whale me	bully-ragged
chimbly	palavering
tear around	roust
hair-ball	sand in my craw
bills	fantods
tanned me	hove
big-bug	truck
hifalut'n	

Section 2
(Chapters XII–XXIII)

sentimentering	seegars
a-booming	sockdolager

Section 3
(Chapters XXIV–XXXI)

slouch	talk like the muggins
beatenest	go the whole hog
flathead	shut of them
dad fetch	doggery
sand in her	yellocution (elocution)
tears and flapdoodle	

Section 4
(Chapters XXXII–XLIII)

howdy-do	purtrified
smouch	counterpin (counterpane)

River Terms

Section 1
(Chapters I–XI)

skiff	river had begun to rise
soundings	rushes
navigate	steamboat

Section 2
(Chapters XII–XXIII)

towhead	pilot house
texas	stern

Vocabulary Activity Ideas

You can help your students learn and retain the vocabulary in *The Adventures of Huckleberry Finn* by providing them with interesting vocabulary activities. Here are some ideas to try.

❑ People of all ages like to make and solve puzzles. Ask your students to make their own **crossword puzzles** or **word search puzzles** using the vocabulary words from the story.

❑ Challenge your students to a **vocabulary bee!** This is similar to a spelling bee, but in addition to spelling each word correctly, the game participants must correctly define the words as well.

❑ Play **vocabulary concentration**. The goal of this game is to match vocabulary words with their definitions. Divide the class into groups of two to five students. Have students make two sets of the cards the same size and color. On one set have them write the vocabulary words. On the second set have them write the definitions. All cards are mixed together and placed face down on a table. A player picks two cards. If the pair matches the word with its definition, the player keeps the cards and takes another turn. If the cards do not match, they are returned to their places face down on the table, and another player takes a turn. Players must concentrate to remember the locations of the words and their definitions. The game continues until all matches have been made. This is an ideal activity for free exploration time.

❑ Have your students practice their writing skills by creating sentences and paragraphs in which multiple vocabulary words are used correctly. Ask them to share their **compact vocabulary** sentences and paragraphs with the class.

❑ Ask your students to create paragraphs which use the vocabulary words to present **history lessons** that relate to the time period of the novel.

❑ Challenge your students to use a specific vocabulary word from the story at least **10 times in one day**. They must keep a record of when, how, and why the word was used.

❑ As a group activity, have students work together to create an **illustrated dictionary** of the vocabulary words.

❑ **Play 20 clues** with the entire class. In this game, one student selects a vocabulary word and gives clues about this word, one by one, until someone in the class can guess the word.

❑ Play **vocabulary charades**. In this game, vocabulary words are acted out.

You probably have many more ideas to add to this list. Try them! See students' vocabulary interest and retention increase.

Quiz—What Do You Know?

Answer the following questions about Chapters I through XI.

1. How did Huck become rich?

_____

_____

2. When Tom and the other boys tell Huck he cannot join the gang because he does not have a family "to kill," what does Huck offer as a solution?

_____

_____

3. Huck sees Pap's footprints in the snow and asks Jim to tell his fortune. Summarize what Jim tells Huck in Chapter IV.

_____

_____

4. Explain what Pap thinks about Huck's living with the widow and going to school.

_____

_____

5. Pap takes Huck to the Illinois side of the Mississippi River where he beats him. How is Huck able to get away from his father?

_____

_____

6. Huck hides on Jackson's Island where he finds the runaway slave, Jim. Why has Jim run away from Miss Watson?

_____

_____

7. What "joke" does Huck play on Jim in Chapter X? What happens to Jim?

_____

_____

8. Why does Huck dress up like a girl and leave Jackson's Island?

_____

_____

9. What is some of the reasoning Mrs. Loftus uses to figure out that Huck is a boy?

_____

_____

10. Why does Huck hurry back to Jackson's Island to tell Jim they must hurry and leave?

_____

_____

Aspects of Wealth

Huck Finn is rich due to the robber's treasure he and Tom Sawyer found. However, he does not have much use for it. In fact, he feels it causes more trouble than it is worth and tries to give it away to the judge in Chapter IV.

Consider what money can and cannot do. Create an art work based on your thinking.

Materials needed:

- 8½ inch (21.25 cm) square white paper
- markers, crayons, and other art supplies
- magazines, scissors, and glue
- 10–inch (25 cm) square pieces of differently colored construction paper
- a roll of wide masking tape

Directions:

1. Draw a line down the center of your square.

2. Place a small picture of yourself on top of the line. (optional)

3. On the left side place drawings or pictures of what you would buy if you were given all the money you could want.

4. On the right side place drawings or pictures of what money cannot buy. Also include things that money might take away.

After finishing, choose a 10-inch square of construction paper to frame your art work.

Use everyone's class piece to form a quilt (with the masking tape) for a classroom wall or to form a border around the room. (Another way to display is to hang each piece over the student's desk, using a string suspended from the ceiling with a clothespin at the end.)

Dialect and Nonstandard English

In Chapter IV, Jim says, "Yo' ole father doan' know yit what he's a-gwyne to do." Would you give this same information using the same words as Jim? Maybe you would say, "Your old dad doesn't know what he will do," or "Your elderly father hasn't made a decision." All of these sentences give the same information. However, the place we were raised and the people we have listened to as children have given us our own special way of speaking.

Dialect is defined as speaking that is characteristic of a certain group or of the people from a certain geographical region. Dialects may differ from one another in the way vocabulary, pronunciation, and grammar are used. In most countries, one dialect has become dominant. In America, this is called *standard English* and can be heard on news broadcasts. Most people, however, speak a different dialect. Some writers like Mark Twain, Langston Hughes, and Mildred Taylor use written dialect in the dialogue of their writings in order to let the reader know how the character would sound.

There are many distinct dialects spoken in the United States. Three of the most familiar are the New England dialect, the New York dialect, and the Southern dialect.

In groups of two or three, read each of the expressions below and determine how it might be said in standard English.

Example: *He was just a-settin' quiet-like* means "He was just sitting quietly."

1. *Didn't aim to tote it the whole way.*   (New England)
2. *Can't for the life of me understand.*   (New England)
3. *He was givin' me the one-two look with his eyes.*   (New York)
4. *He's the type person who lies.*   (New York)
5. *He run off ever which way.*   (Southern)
6. *If I had my druthers, I'd go.*   (Southern)

Pick out five examples of dialect from the *The Adventures of Huckleberry Finn*. Write them down and have your group put them into standard English.

1. _____

   _____

2. _____

   _____

3. _____

   _____

4. _____

   _____

5. _____

   _____

Reading Response Journals

One great way to ensure that the reading of *The Adventures of Huckleberry Finn* becomes a personal experience for each student is to include the use of Reading Response Journals in your plans. In these journals, students can be encouraged to respond to the story in a number of ways. Here are a few ideas.

❑ Tell them that the purpose of the journal is to record their thoughts, ideas, observations, and questions as they read *The Adventures of Huckleberry Finn.*

❑ Provide students with, or ask them to suggest, topics from the story that would stimulate writing. Here are a few examples from the chapters in Section 1:

   • Life with an abusive parent is difficult whether it is in 1850 or today. However, there are fewer places a child can run away to in the modern world. If Huck were living today, where do you think he might go?

   • When Jim runs away, he must live in fear because the white people see him as the property of Miss Watson. Even though there is no slavery in the United States today, many people are still treated unequally. Why do some people treat others with hate and distrust?

   • In order to survive, Huck must live "by his wits." How do you think you would do if you were suddenly forced to live on your own? What are some of the experiences you have had that would show why you might succeed or fail?

❑ After the reading of each chapter, students can write one or more new things they learned in the chapter.

❑ Have students use a double-entry journal by writing one short quote that interests them from each chapter on the left of their paper. On the right side they should express their own ideas about the quote. Ask students to draw their responses to certain events or characters in the story, using blank pages in their journals.

❑ Tell students that they may use their journals to record "diary-type" responses that they may want to enter.

❑ Give students quotes from the novel and ask them to write their own responses. Make sure to do this before you go over the quotations in class. In groups they could list the different ways students can respond to the same quote.

❑ Allow students time to write in their journals daily.

❑ Personal reflections will be read by the teacher, but no corrections or letter grades will be assigned. Credit is given for effort, and all students who sincerely try will be awarded credit. If a grade is desired for this type of entry, grade according to the number of journal entries completed. For example, if five journal assignments were made and the student conscientiously completes all five, then he or she receives an "A."

❑ Nonjudgmental teacher responses should be made to let the students know you enjoy their journals. Here are some types of responses that will please your journal writers and encourage them to write more.

   • "You have really found what's important in the story!"

   • "You write so clearly, I almost feel as if I am there."

   • "If you feel comfortable, I'd like you to share this with the class. I think they'll enjoy it as much as I have."

Humor

Mark Twain states in the "Notice" that persons attempting to find a moral in this book will be banished. While he slightly overstates his case, we should not forget that this novel is very funny. It is important to allow students to find the humor in the novel. Too often readers are so concerned with the social aspect that they forget to look for what is funny.

I. Finding Finn's Funnies

The Adventures of Huckleberry Finn is a funny book, but too often readers miss what is funny when they cannot hear it aloud. Make a chart of the parts that you find humorous.

Example:

Quote	Character Who Is Speaking	Comments
Chapter I "She called me a lot of other names, too, but she never meant no harm by it."	Huck	The widow uses words that aren't "nice" when she is angry at Huck.
Chapter II "I offered them Miss Watson."	Huck	Huck is happy to allow the gang to kill Miss Watson because he doesn't like her anyway.

II. Jokes

Humor is an important element of American culture. It fits in with our optimistic viewpoint. Why not begin each day of your study of *Huck Finn* with a humorous story or cartoon from the newspaper? Humor books are easily obtained at the library. Humor is an excellent way to tap into higher-level thinking skills since the ability to understand it tends to be complex.

You might have each student bring in a joke or cartoon to share with the class. A word of caution: Listen to each joke the day before to "OK" it for content. Here is an excellent way to teach the class the type of humor appropriate in a classroom.

Quiz—What Do You Know?

Answer the following questions about Chapters XII through XXIII.

1. On the back of this paper, briefly summarize the Grangerford episode or the Boggs-Sherburn episode.

2. How do Huck and Jim avoid being seen as they are floating down the river?

   _____

   _____

3. Why are Jim and Huck looking for the town of Cairo (Kay-ro), Illinois?

   _____

   _____

4. Why is Huck having trouble deciding to help Jim escape to freedom?

   _____

   _____

5. What is one of the stories Huck makes up to avoid trouble?

   _____

   _____

6. Satire is a device used to make fun of the way people act. What do you feel Mark Twain is saying about people when he uses satire to describe the Grangerfords?

   _____

   _____

7. What is one of the quotes from Chapter XVIII to show Huck is happy to be back on the raft? (Don't forget to use quotation marks.)

   _____

   _____

8. What is one of the statements that Colonel Sherburn makes to the lynching mob that makes them go home?

   _____

   _____

9. What are some of the ways the king and the duke speak and act that tell the reader that these men are lying about their past?

   _____

   _____

10. How does Jim show that he is a good parent when he speaks about his daughter?

   _____

   _____

Predicting the Outcome

By the end of Chapter XXIII, Huck has been through many adventures along the Mississippi River. At this point he and Jim have passed the mouth of the Ohio River, so they must continue down the river. (A non-motorized vessel cannot go up the river against the current.) The king and the duke are aboard the raft. Huck has no real plans. He just goes where the river takes him and reacts to each new adventure.

What will happen next? Before reading, consider how you might continue the novel. Use some of the information Twain has given the reader. Make sure to include the four characters—Huck, Jim, the king, and the duke in your answer.

After you write, practice reading your version with dramatic feeling. When it sounds close to perfect, put it on tape. Play it for the class.

_____

_____

_____

_____

_____

_____

_____

_____

_____

_____

_____

_____

_____

_____

Living on a Raft

After Huck barely escapes with his life from the Grangerford-Shepherdson's feud, he and Jim have some wonderful days floating down the river. In Chapter XIX, Huck says:

> *Two or three days and nights went by; I reckon I might say they swum by, they slid along so quiet and smooth and lovely . . . . Then we set out the lines. Next we slid into the river and had a swim . . . .Not a sound anywheres—perfectly still—just like the whole world was asleep . . . . Sometimes we'd have that whole river all to ourselves for the longest time. Yonder was the banks and the islands, across the water . . . maybe you could hear a fiddle or a song coming over from one of them . . . . It's lovely to live on a raft. We had the sky up there, all speckled with stars, and we used to lay on our backs and look up at them . . . .*

In a group discuss the items below. After discussing, each person should record his or her own responses on their paper. When you are finished, compare and contrast your responses with those of other groups.

❑ What images does this excerpt from the book bring to your imagination?

_____

_____

❑ Does it remind you of anything you have experienced?

_____

_____

❑ If you had the opportunity, do you think you would enjoy an experience similar to the one Huck describes? Why?

_____

_____

❑ What would be most fun about a raft trip down a river?

_____

_____

❑ What might be a major problem of such a trip?

_____

_____

❑ When *Huck Finn* was published in 1884, young readers thought this type of trip sounded wonderful. Do you think most young people would feel the same today? Explain your thoughts.

_____

_____

"It's Lovely to Live on a Raft"

The title of this activity is the sentence Huck uses to sum up his feelings as he and Jim are floating down the Mississippi. Read the first few pages of Chapter XIX where Twain writes poetically about life on the river. In the frame below, draw your interpretation of what Huck describes in this section of the novel. You probably will want to place the raft in your picture. Pay close attention to the colors of the sky.

Living on Your Own

Huckleberry Finn elects to run away several times in the novel. Although he has little choice, he knows it means he must live on his own.

Answer these questions about living alone.

1. The first time Huck runs away, it is from his father. Do you think Huck makes the right decision? Why or why not?

   _____

   _____

   _____

2. Most people who run away are looking for something they do not have. What is Huck looking for?

   _____

   _____

   _____

3. What would be the advantages of living on your own?

   _____

   _____

   _____

4. What would be some of the disadvantages of living on your own?

   _____

   _____

   _____

5. What are the dangers of living on your own?

   _____

   _____

   _____

6. What are some other options to consider before a person feels it necessary to run away from home?

   _____

   _____

   _____

Quiz—What Do You Know?

Answer the following questions about Chapters XXIV through XXXI.

1. On the back of this paper, briefly summarize the Wilks episode.

2. When Huck says "It was enough to make a body ashamed of the human race," what is he talking about?

   _____

   _____

3. Who is the only one at the Wilks' home who realizes that the king and the duke are frauds? Why do you feel this person is the only one who realizes the truth?

   _____

   _____

4. Why does Huck decide to steal the money? Where is he forced to hide the gold?

   _____

   _____

5. Mary Jane is very concerned about the slaves. Why?

   _____

   _____

6. Why is it necessary to dig up Peter Wilks' body?

   _____

   _____

7. After the body is dug up, how is Huck able to escape and get back to the raft?

   _____

   _____

8. What horrible action does the king take toward Jim?

   _____

   _____

9. What is one of the problems Huck faces when he hears about what happened to Jim?

   _____

   _____

10. What convinces Huck to steal Jim, even though he feels it is the wrong thing to do?

   _____

   _____

Making Candy

Huckleberry Finn takes place during a time when almost all cooking was done in the home. This would include any sweets or desserts. Most young people today get candy from their local supermarkets, but only a few have actually made some. Here are two recipes popular in the area where Huck lived. You can make them at home or in your classroom.

Here is one that requires no cooking.

Honey Candy

- 1 cup (240 mL) instant nonfat dry milk
- 1 cup plain or chunky peanut butter
- 1 cup honey
- ¹/₂ teaspoon (2.5 mL) vanilla

Mix together all ingredients and shape into balls or shapes. Refrigerate before serving. Yield: Approximately 24 pieces.

The next one is more complicated—and even more fun.

Saltwater Taffy

- 1 ¹/₄ pounds (560 g) sugar
- 1 ¹/₄ pounds (600 mL) white corn syrup
- 2 cups (480) water
- 1 tablespoon (15 mL) butter
- 2 tablespoons (30 mL) salt
- ¹/₂ teaspoon (2.5 mL) flavoring (maple, almond, peppermint, lemon, vanilla, etc.)
- Food coloring

Put sugar, syrup, and water in a saucepan and stir until boiling begins. Continue boiling, but do not stir. A thread will appear. Remove pan from heat, add butter and salt, and pour into buttered platters. When cool enough—pull! Add flavoring and coloring while pulling. Cut into pieces and wrap each piece in waxed paper.

Making It Up!

In Chapter XXVIII, Huck makes up a story about Mary Jane Wilks going to care for a sick friend. He does this because he feels the truth will get Mary Jane and her sisters, Joanna and Susan, into trouble. Huck makes up many stories in the course of his travels down the Mississippi River. Most readers would say that he only makes up stories to protect others and, sometimes, himself.

In this activity, work with one or two other class members to write the reason Huck makes up the following stories:

1. Huck tells Mrs. Loftus in Chapter XI that his name is Sarah (or Mary!) Williams, and "her" mother is sick, and the family is out of money and food.

   _____

   _____

   _____

2. In Chapter XVI, Huck makes some men on the river think that his family has smallpox.

   _____

   _____

3. Huck tells the king and the duke in Chapter XX that his pa and brother drowned on a trip down the river, but he and the servant Jim were able to swim to safety.

   _____

   _____

   _____

4. In Chapter XXVII, Huck tells the king and the duke that the gold was stolen by some slaves owned by the Wilks.

   _____

   _____

   _____

5. Can your group think of another story Huck makes up to protect himself or someone else?

   _____

   _____

   _____

6. Does your group think that Huck's stories can be justified, or is he just plain lying? Defend your decision with reasons.

   _____

   _____

   _____

Mississippi River Facts

Directions: Use appropriate reference books to locate the following information about the Mississippi River.

1. In the Chippewa language, *Misi Sipi* means_____.

2. The length of the river is approximately_____ km or_____ miles.

3. The main tributary of the Mississippi is the_____.

4. The first European to see the Mississippi was a Spaniard,_____,who called it the Rio Grande (Big River).

5. Although two Frenchmen, Louis Jolliet and Jacques Marquette, went down the river to what is now Arkansas in 1673, the first European to get credit for sailing the whole length of the river (in 1681) is another Frenchman,_____.

6. The source of the river in Minnesota is Lake_____.

7. The "Twin Cities" on the northern part of the river are_____ and_____.

8. Mark Twain was born in the small city of_____, 150 miles north of St. Louis, Missouri.

9. The famous landmark on the river (in the city of St. Louis) is the_____Arch.

10. The river which joins the Mississippi right below Cairo, Illinois, is the_____.

11. The large Tennessee city on the river is_____.

12. The large body of water the Mississippi empties into is the_____.

13. The delta area of the river is next to the city of_____.

14. The 10 U.S. states that border the Mississippi are . . .

_____   _____

_____   _____

_____

_____

_____

_____

Making Choices

Throughout the novel, Huck is making choices. Consider the following problems that Huck faces and then write your responses to them.

1. Huck decides to go back to Jackson's Island in order to tell Jim the bounty hunters are after him. Why does Huck return to get Jim? What do you think Huck is thinking as he crosses the river from Mrs. Loftus' house to Jackson's Island?

_____

_____

_____

_____

_____

2. Huck must decide if he will help Jim escape to the free territory. He has learned that black people in the South are considered property. If he helps Jim escape, then he is helping to steal someone's property. How do you feel about what Huck is doing? Explain why you feel this way.

_____

_____

_____

_____

_____

3. Huck, in Chapter XVI, lies in order to keep some men from finding Jim. Even though Huck worries about his decisions, the reader sees that Huck is doing the right thing. Explain why Huck is having trouble deciding what to do.

_____

_____

_____

_____

4. Huck tells Mary Jane Wilks that the king and duke are pretending to be her uncles in order to steal the gold. Why do you think it takes Huck so long to decide to tell Mary Jane? Why does it become more difficult for someone to confess as more time passes?

_____

_____

_____

_____

Quiz—What Do You Know?

Answer the following questions about Chapters XXXII through XLIII.

1. On the back of this paper, briefly summarize Chapters XXXII and XLIII.

2. How is Jim able to get his revenge on the king and the duke?

_____

_____

3. What do the people of Pikesville do to the king and the duke? How does Huck feel about it?

_____

_____

4. How would you compare Huck's attitude with Tom's concerning Jim's escape?

_____

_____

5. What is ironic about the way that Tom and Huck get the grindstone into the hut?

_____

_____

6. When Tom is shot, what does Jim's behavior say about his character?

_____

_____

7. What does the doctor say about Jim to the men holding him?

_____

_____

8. What has happened to Huck's father?

_____

_____

9. At the end of the novel, what surprising occurrence causes Jim to be freed?

_____

_____

10. What does Huck plan to do as the novel ends? Why?

_____

_____

Travel Brochure

If Huck had gone to a travel agency before starting his trip down the Mississippi, there would have been no way that the agent could have planned such an exciting trip. But if such a trip could have been planned, imagine how the travel brochure might have looked.

In this activity, write and illustrate a travel brochure that shows some of the sights Huck saw and the activities in which he participated. Anything that is in the novel can be discussed or pictured. (Be careful about the Royal Nonesuch, however!) Perhaps your teacher will bring in some travel brochures or you could visit a local agency and ask for one or two of them.

Supplies:

- an 11" x 14½" (27.5 cm x 36.25 cm) sheet of blank white paper
- markers, crayons, and paint
- rulers and pencils

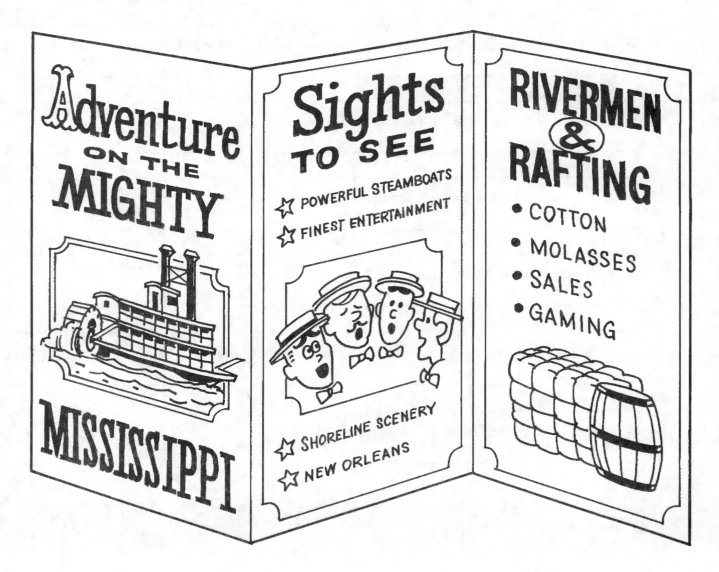

Adult Confusion

Much of the fun of the novel's last section consists of Tom and Huck confusing Aunt Sally. The poor woman is so bewildered that she thinks she might be losing her mind. Many young people consider this to be the funniest part of the book.

Work with a partner to create a story about two children who confuse an adult. Make it as much fun and as convoluted as what Tom and Huck do to Aunt Sally. One way to begin is to brainstorm ideas. Think of real situations in which you have been involved or have heard about. Or begin with a story, movie, or TV plot, and add your own special touches.

Have fun and really confuse the poor adult!

_____

_____

_____

_____

_____

_____

_____

_____

_____

_____

_____

_____

_____

_____

_____

_____

Songs of the Period

One way to help students understand the time *Huck Finn* takes place is to hear some of the songs of the time. Much of the essence of the culture of the United States can be found in its popular songs. Students will enjoy knowing the kinds of songs heard on the riverboats and in the theaters of the pre-Civil War period.

I. Stephen Foster, America's most famous song writer of the nineteenth century, wrote many of his compositions around the time of Huck's journey down the Mississippi River. Certainly passengers on the paddlewheelers would have been hearing his famous melodies. The music is easily obtainable at your local library.

"Oh, Susanna"

Chorus
Oh! Susanna, don't you cry for me;
I come from Alabama, with my banjo on my knee.

Verses
I come from Alabama with a banjo on my knee;
I'm goin' to Lou-siana my true love for to see.
It rained all night the day I left, the weather it was dry;
The sun so hot I froze to death, Susanna don't you cry.
I had a dream the other night, when everything was still
I thought I saw Susanna dear, a-comin' down the hill.
The buckwheat cake was in her mouth, the tear was in her eye,
Said I, I'm comin' from the south
Susanna don't you cry.
I soon will be in New Orleans, and then I'll look all 'round
And when I find Susanna, I'll fall upon the ground.
But if I do not find her, this man'll surely die,
And when I'm dead and buried,
Susanna don't you cry.

Other Stephen Foster favorites include "Jeanie With the Light Brown Hair" and "Camptown Races."

II.   Some older songs still popular during Huck's day were these:

"Froggie Went A-Courtin"
(a sample of its many verses)
Oh, Froggie went a-courtin' and he did ride,
uh-huh, uh-huh.
Froggie went a courtin' and he did ride,
A sword and pistol by his side, uh-huh, uh-huh.
He rode up to Miss Mousie's door uh-huh, uh-huh.
He rode up to Miss Mousie's door.
Where he had often been before, uh-huh, uh-huh.
He took Miss Mousie on his knee, uh-huh, uh-huh.
He took Miss Mousie on his knee,
And said, "Miss Mouse, will you marry me?" uh-huh, uh-huh.

"Shenandoah"
Oh, Shen-an-doah, I long to hear you.
Away, you rolling river!
Oh, Shenandoah, I long to hear you,
Away, I'm bound away,
Cross the wide Missouri.

III. There is a modern musical version of the novel called *Big River* with music and lyrics by Roger Miller. The CD or tape is available. Your students would enjoy hearing the numbers. Preview first.

What You Do Best

Huckleberry Finn is able to do many things well. He can fish, navigate a raft, and take care of himself. He also has the ability to understand other people's problems and is able to change his attitude as he learns more about Jim. He seems like a person that most kids would like to call a friend.

Everyone has the ability to do many things well.

- What do you do well?
- What can you do that almost no one else in your class can do?
- What do you know about which only a few people or perhaps no one else in your class knows about?

You might be thinking, "I really don't know what to write. I can't do much." Think of Huck—he feels the same about himself. Yet he has many special abilities. So do you!

Make an I AM booklet.

1. Cut four or five sheets of notebook paper down the center, lengthwise.

2. For the front and back, make a cover of construction paper that is just a bit wider than the notebook paper.

3. Staple the notebook paper inside the construction paper.

4. Write I AM (which stands for "INTERESTING, AWESOME ME!") on the cover.

5. Open to the first sheet and start listing all the things you can do and your special qualities.

6. As you think of more during the next week, continue your list. Don't be satisfied until you reach at least 100.

Don't think you can do it? Yes, you can. You just don't realize how many great qualities you have. Are you a good friend? Write it down. Do you understand what you read? Write it down. Can you figure out word problems? Do you help with chores at home? Can you cook? Play a musical instrument? Dance? Saw a board?

Life Experiences

Huck learns about life as he travels down the Mississippi River. Each time a new incident occurs and Huck responds to it in words or actions, he is educated by his life experiences.

What do the following episodes contribute to Huck's education about life?

A. The rattlesnake biting Jim

_____

_____

_____

_____

_____

B. The Grangerford feud

_____

_____

_____

_____

_____

C. The king and duke trying to steal the Wilks' gold

_____

_____

_____

_____

_____

D. Jim's concern for his daughter

_____

_____

_____

_____

_____

Any Questions?

When you finished reading *Huck Finn*, did you have some questions that were left unanswered? Write them here.

_____

_____

_____

_____

_____

Then work in groups or by yourself to prepare possible answers for the questions you have asked above or those written below. When you have finished, share your ideas with the class.

❑ Does Huck return with Aunt Polly to St. Petersburg?

 If he does . . .

- what kind of student is he?
- what does he do after school hours?
- will he graduate?
- what does Huck do for a job after he leaves school?
- will he continue to let Tom Sawyer lead him around, or does he start believing in himself?

❑ Does Huck "light out for the territory"?

 If he does . . .

- where does he end up living?
- how does he support himself?
- what sorts of adventures will he have?

❑ Do Huck and Jim stay together?

❑ Does Huck understand that all black people are entitled to the same respect which he realized Jim deserved?

❑ When will Huck fall in love? What kind of girl would he be interested in?

❑ Will he ever meet the king or duke again?

❑ Will he ever visit the Wilks girls?

Book Report Ideas

There are many ways to report on a book. After you have finished reading *The Adventures of Huckleberry Finn*, choose one method of reporting that interests you. It may be a way your teacher suggests, an idea of your own, or one of the ways mentioned below.

❑ **See What I Read?**

This report is visual. A model of a scene from the story can be created, or a likeness of one or more of the characters from the story can be drawn or sculpted.

❑ **Time Capsule**

This report provides people living in the future with the reasons *The Adventures of Huckleberry Finn* is such an outstanding book. Make a time-capsule design and neatly print or write your reasons inside the capsule. You may wish to "bury" your capsule after you have shared it with your classmates. Perhaps one day someone will find it and read *Huckleberry Finn* because of what you wrote.

❑ **Come to Life!**

This report lends itself to a group project. A size-appropriate group prepares a scene from the story for dramatization, acts it out, and relates the significance of the scene to the entire book. Costumes and props will add to the dramatization.

❑ **Who or What?**

This report is similar to "20 Questions." The reporter gives a series of clues about a character from the story in vague-to-precise, general-to-specific order. After all clues have been given, the identity of the mystery character must be deduced. After the character has been identified, the same reporter presents another "20 Clues" about an event in the story.

❑ **A Character Comes to Life!**

Suppose one of the characters in *Huckleberry Finn* came to life and walked into your home or classroom. This report gives a view of what this characters sees, hears, and feels as he or she experiences the world in which you live.

❑ **Sales Talk**

This report serves as an advertisement to "sell" *Huckleberry Finn* to one or more specific groups. You decide on the group to target and the sales pitch you will use. Include some kind of graphics in your presentation.

❑ **Literary Interview**

This report is done in pairs. One student will pretend to be a character in the story, steeped completely in the persona of his or her character. The other student will play the role of a television or radio interviewer, trying to provide the audience with insights into the character's personality and life. It is the responsibility of the partners to create meaningful questions and appropriate responses.

❑ **Historical**

Consider one of your interests. Research the way that interest or a related one was interpreted in 1850, the year the novel is set. Report to the class. Some possible topics—food, entertainment, transportation, politics (pre-Civil War concerns), lives of the people.

Research Activity

The duke, in Chapter XX, says he most enjoys the "histrionic muse," which is a fancy way of saying he enjoys performing. He goes to small towns up and down the river, acting in scenes from famous plays. Twain makes it clear that the duke knows very little about the plays he is doing, but the people on the river know even less. Before there was any electronic entertainment (movies, TV, radio) people relied on live performers. Citizens of little towns were so starved for entertainment they would even go to see "The Royal Nonesuch."

Consider your ideas about entertainment and then plan a show for your class.

❑ What is your definition of entertainment?

❑ What kind of television program do you like best? Why?

❑ Have you seen a movie lately that you really enjoyed? What was it and what made it special?

❑ Do you listen to music on the radio or have a tape or CD player? What is your favorite kind of music?

❑ Have you been to a sports event in the past year? What was it? What did you enjoy most about it?

❑ Have you ever seen a live performance (besides a sporting event)? What was it and what did you like about it? If you go often to see plays or musicals, explain what makes them different from movies and TV shows.

River Boat Research—Show Time

You may want to do some research on the types of shows done on the Mississippi River boats of the 19th century. Choose from the following list of entertainments common to that time. (No video—do it live!)

- a story
- a poem
- a skit
- a tap dance
- a speech
- a song
- a scene from a melodrama

Think before you begin:

❑ Should it be original or should I adapt it?

❑ What would the class enjoy seeing?

❑ How long should it be?

❑ What would I enjoy doing for them?

❑ Should I do this by myself or get a classmate to help me?

❑ What equipment will I need? (stage, scripts, costumes, etc.)

Discuss with your teacher an appropriate time to present your entertainment to the class.

What Has Huck Learned?

Huck Finn learns about human nature during his journey through the novel. Each new idea or concept is taught by an experience the young boy has. In the chart below, explain what Huck learned or describe the learning experience which taught him.

What Huck Has Learned	The Learning Experience
Practical jokes are not always funny. You must consider the consequences of your actions.	
	Pap locks Huck up in a cabin and refuses to allow him to return to the Widow Douglas or to continue his education.
Appearances can be deceiving (or, to use an idiom, you can't judge a book by its cover.)	
	Colonel Sherburn is able to disperse the crowd by "explaining" how cowardly they are acting. The men forget about the lynching and return home.
Some people are very gullible (will easily believe others), even when it does not seem logical for them to believe those who are lying and cheating them.	
Things which society teaches you don't always make sense in practical situations.	
	Huck tells Mary Jane the truth about the king and duke so she will not be worried about the slaves being separated from their families.

Jim's View

Although the novel is told from Huck's point of view, the reader can also understand what Jim is going through on his trip down the Mississippi River.

Consider the following:

1. What is one of Jim's happiest experiences as he travels down the river? Explain the reasons for your answer.

2. What is one of Jim's worst experiences? Explain the reasons for your choice.

3. What is going through Jim's mind during the Grangerford-Shepherdson's episode?

4. Explain why you feel Jim has such different views on King Solomon than Huck has.

5. What are some of the major differences in the way Jim is viewing his experiences and the way Huck views his experiences?

6. What do you think Jim's view of Huck is when he first encounters him on Jackson's Island? How does it change as the novel progresses?

7. Suppose Jim is the narrator of the novel. What will be some of the differences in the way the events are told?

8. Do you feel Mark Twain would have understood enough about Jim's viewpoint to write the novel with him as the narrator, or would Jim's novel need to be written by a black writer?

9. Would students from different cultures have a different view of this novel? How would a black student view the novel differently from a white student? Why?

10. As an expression of your own cultural identity, write a paragraph on your response to the novel. Explain what it is about your identity that makes you respond to the novel as you do.

Essay

Expository

If you want your students to write essays on a prepared topic, you will want to give them as much help as you can. Let them know early (before finishing the book) what your topic choices will be. This will enable them to look for possible support as they read. As they read, ask them questions which will help elicit supporting ideas.

The following are two essay topics you might use. Both would require a close reading of the novel.

1. Discuss what you feel is the most important lesson Huck Finn learned from his experiences. (Include how he learned this lesson and how it changed his thinking.)

2. Some critics have said Jim is Huck's true father. Discuss what this means. (Include what Jim taught Huck.)

After they have read about two-thirds of the novel, you might want the students to decide on which of the two characters they wish to concentrate. As they read the last 10 or 15 chapters, have them consider some or all of the following as a lead-up to the essay.

❑ What does your character think of himself?

❑ What is your character most afraid of?

❑ What does he think of the people of St. Petersburg?

❑ What is the major decision he faces in the novel?

❑ What are some of the choices he has?

❑ Why does your character make the choice he does? (Deciding not to choose is also a choice.)

❑ Why does your character believe that his choice is the right one?

❑ Does your character consider the consequences when he makes the choice?

❑ Does your character's choice change his personality or values?

Essay *(cont.)*

Personal

If you wish your students to write essays based on experiences from their own lives and connect them to the novel, you might consider the following questions to develop a topic.

1. Think of a time when you were doing something you were not supposed to do. Were you caught? How did you try to get yourself out of trouble? Did it work?
2. Can you recall a time you felt right about doing something you were told was wrong? Did you act on your feeling? What was the result?
3. Describe a situation when you got carried away in a crowd and did something you would not have done had you been alone. (Or have you ever witnessed a group do something that they probably would not have done if they acted as individuals?)
4. Have you ever had to rely on someone else to help you solve a problem? Did the other person come through for you? Was your faith in the other person justified?
5. Has there been a time when you have hurt someone you love or really care about? What did you do to regain his or her affection? Did you carefully plan and carry it out? How long did it take for things to feel normal again?
6. Have you ever wanted something very much that was denied to you? Why weren't you allowed to have it? What has this experience taught you?

When your students have chosen their topics, you might have them connect the novel to their lives as part of their thesis and support. An example of a thesis paragraph:

> *When my parents told me they were getting a divorce, I was completely devastated. I wanted them so much to stay together. Like Jim, who tried to get to Cairo in order to be free, I tried to do what I could to keep them together. I understand what it means, like Jim, to want something so desperately which you are not able to obtain. Your life experiences, especially traumatic ones, can make a big difference in your view of life.*

You might want to let your students choose the expository topic or the personal one. Since students do not all learn in the same way, some might prefer doing one type of essay over the other.

Unit Test

Multiple Choice (Circle the answer that best completes the statement.)

1. At the beginning of the novel, Huck lived with . . .

    A) Aunt Polly.   C) his father.

    B) Widow Douglas.

2. Jim runs away from St. Petersburg because . . .

    A) he is tired of being a slave.   C) he is afraid of being sold down the river.

    B) his daughter has been stolen.

3. One major reason Huck has trouble accepting Jim as an equal is . . .

    A) Jim has been cruel to Huck in the past.

    B) Huck has been taught that blacks are inferior to whites.

    C) Tom and Jim once tried to cheat Huck out of the his $6,000.

4. Which of the following would be a true statement about the way Twain saw his main character? Huck . . .

    A) was far more intelligent than other boys his age.

    B) had a wonderful sense of humor.

    C) was forced to be practical because of his difficult life.

    D) always believed what he was told by others.

5. Which of the following was not true about Huck and Jim's relationship?

    A) Jim cared for Huck before Huck was sympathetic toward Jim.

    B) Huck never enjoyed the results of the practical jokes he played on Jim.

    C) Huck never felt Jim was being sincere about his friendship.

    D) Jim cared for Huck as much as a father would care for his son.

Matching (Match the character with what he/she does.)

_____ Huck   A. sold Jim for 40 dollars.

_____ Jim   B. officially gave Jim his freedom.

_____ Tom Sawyer   C. had trouble understanding how spoons, shirts, and sheets
                                             kept disappearing.

_____ King

_____ Sophia Grangerford   D. was almost always practical and used common sense.

_____ Aunt Sally   E. enjoyed adventures even if they hurt others.

_____ Miss Watson   F. asked Huck to get a Bible from the church.

                                          G. enjoyed telling fortunes.

Sequence (Put these events in order by number (1 to 5) on the lines.

_____ Huck decides to "go to hell" for Jim.

_____ Huck and Jim leave Jackson's Island.

_____ Huck makes Jim think that getting lost in the fog was a dream.

_____ Huck puts the dead snake in Jim's blanket.

_____ Huck writes a letter to Miss Watson telling her that Jim is locked up on the Phelps' farm.

Response

Explain the meaning of each of these quotations from *Huckleberry Finn.*

Chapter II: *"When he was ten foot off Tom whispered to me, and wanted to tie Jim to the tree for fun. But I said no; he might wake and make a disturbance, and then they'd find out I wasn't in."*

Chapter III: *"I was so ignorant, and so kind of low-down and ornery."*

Chapter V: *"Oh, yes, this is a wonderful government, wonderful."*

Chapter VIII: *"Well, I did. I said I wouldn't and I'll stick to it. Honest injun, I will. People would call me a low-down Abolitionist and despise me for keeping mum—but that don't make no difference."*

Chapter IX: *"It's a dead man. Yes, indeedy; naked too. He's been shot in de back. I reck'n he's been dead two or three days. Come in, Huck, but don't look at his face—it's too gashly."*

Chapter X: *"I wasn't going to let Jim find out it (the snake skin) was all my fault, not if I could help it."*

Chapter XII: *"Git up and hump yourself, Jim! There ain't a minute to lose. They're after us!"*

Chapter XV: *"I didn't do him no more mean tricks, and I wouldn't done that one if I'd a knew it would make him feel that way."*

Chapter XVI: *"I see I was weakening; so I just give up trying, and up and says: He's white."*

Chapter XVI: *"So it was all up with Cairo."*

Chapter XVIII: *"You feel mighty free and easy and comfortable on a raft."*

Chapter XXII: *"Then the ringmaster he see how he had been fooled, and he was the sickest ringmaster you ever see . . . I wouldn't been in that ringmaster's place, not for a thousand dollars."*

Chapter XXIII: *"Oh, she was plumb deef and dumb, Huck, plumb deef en dumb—en I'd been a treating her so!"*

Chapter XXV: *"Keep your hands off me! You talk like an Englishman, don't you? It's the worst imitation I ever heard . . . You're a fraud, that's what you are."*

Chapter XXVIII: *"She said the beautiful trip to England was most about spoiled for her . . . knowing the mother and the children wasn't ever going to see each other no more."*

Chapter XXXI: *"You can't pray a life."*

Chapter XXXIII: *"Human beings can be awful cruel to one another."*

Chapter XL: *"I doan' budge a step outen dis place 'dout a doctor; not if it's forty years!"*

Chapter the Last: *"But I reckon I got to light out for the territory ahead of the rest, because Aunt Sally she's going to adopt me and sivilize me, and I can't stand it. I been there before."*

Conversations

Work in size-appropriate groups to write and perform the conversations that might have occured in each of the situations below. (You can also use these for brainstorming and think of your own situations for conversation.)

❑ Huck decides to return to St. Petersburg with Aunt Polly and Tom. Write a conversation Huck and Tom have on the day they graduate from high school.

❑ Huck does sneak out for the territory. He comes back to St. Petersburg when he is 20. Write a dialogue between Huck and Tom when they see each other again.

❑ Jim and Huck meet again as old men. Consider what might have happened to them in the intervening years and write a dialogue between two old friends. What do you think their attitudes might be? What might have happened to them? How would they talk about old times—i.e., the adventures in the novel?

❑ Write a dialogue between Jim and a black man or woman at the end of the twentieth century, discussing how much things have changed and/or stayed the same.

❑ Write a dialogue showing Huck and Jim discussing the rights and wrongs of the Colonel Sherburn episode. The conversation should cover the part where Sherburn shoots the drunken man who was insulting him in the street and also the later part when Sherburn faces down the mob that comes to hang him. Is Sherburn a brave man? Are the mob members cowards? Did the drunk man deserve what happened to him? What was the honorable thing to do at each step of these actions? (Consider Jim's rather unconventional but very human reaction to the King Solomon story when you express his reactions to the Sherburn situation.)

❑ For helping Jim escape, Huck is arrested by a sheriff who does not know of Miss Watson's will. Made to stand trial before a judge and jury, Huck hires a lawyer to defend him. Write the lawyer's questions and Huck's answers for Huck's session in the witness chair.

❑ If Huck had children (one boy and one girl) and was telling them about his adventures, what would their questions be and what would Huck's answers be? How could he explain himself and some of his decisions so that he sets a good example for his children?

❑ Years after their adventures, pretend you are interviewing Huck and Jim for a newspaper report on racism. Ask them what their observations and opinions are about the causes of racism and suggestions they might have to eliminate it in this country. (Remember that although neither Huck nor Jim are educated men, they both often show great wisdom and common sense.)

Racism!
A nonviolent solution

Bibliography of Related Reading

Fiction

Twain, Mark. *The Adventures of Tom Sawyer.* Penguin, 1982.

———. *A Connecticut Yankee in King Arthur's Court.* Bantam, 1988.

———. *The Prince and the Pauper.* Penguin, 1989.

———. *Pudd'n head Wilson.* Airmont, 1966.

———. *Tom Sawyer, Detective.* Airmont, 1970.

Other Fiction About the United States in the 19th Century

Reeder, Carolyn. *Shades of Gray.* Macmillan, 1989.

Rinaldi, Ann. *The Last Silk Dress.* Holiday, 1988.

Shore, Laura Jan. *The Sacred Moon Tree.* Bradbury, 1986.

Smucker, Barbara. *Runaway to Freedom: A Story of the Underground Railway.* Harper, 1979.

Tolliver, Ruby. *Muddy Banks.* Texas Christian University, 1986.

Wisler, G. Clifton. *Thunder on the Tennessee.* Dutton, 1983.

Modern Fiction Adventures and Survival Stories

Blackwood, Gary L. *Wild Timothy.* Macmillan, 1987.

Bunting, Eve. *Someone Is Hiding on Alcatraz Island.* Clarion, 1984.

Cazzola, Gus. *To Touch the Deer.* Westminster, 1981.

George, Jean Craighead. *Julie of the Wolves.* Harper, 1972.

Hallman, Ruth. *Search Without Fear.* Putnam, 1987.

Holman, Felice. *Slake's Limbo.* Macmillan, 1974.

Klein, Norma. *Bizou.* Fawcett, 1987.

Lasenby, Jack. *The Lake.* Oxford University Press, 1989.

Major, Kevin. *Hold Fast.* Dell, 1980.

Mazer, Harry. *Snow Bound.* Dell, 1975.

Morey, Walt. *Angry Waters.* Blue Heron, 1990.

Paulsen, Gary. *Hatchet.* Macmillan, 1987.

Ross, Rhea Beth. *The Bet's On, Lizzie Bingman!* Houghton, 1988.

Taylor, Theodore. *The Cay.* Doubleday, 1969.

Nonfiction

Agay, Dennis. *Best Loved Songs of the American People.* Doubleday, 1975.

Bloom, Harold (education). *Mark Twain—Modern Critical Views.* Chelsea House, 1986.

Darrell-Brown Susan. *The Mississippi.* Wayland/Silver Burdett, 1979.

Dudden, Arthur Power. *American Humor.* Oxford University Press, 1987.

Evitts, William J. *Captive Bodies, Free Spirits: The Story of Southern Slavery.* Messner, 1985.

Freedman, Florence. *Two Tickets to Freedom: The True Story of Ellen & William Craft, Fugutive Slaves.* Bedrick, 1989.

Gerber, John C. *Mark Twain.* Twayne Publishers, 1988.

Lomax, Alan. *The Folk Songs of North America.* Doubleday, 1960.

Page, Linda Garland and Eliot Wigginton (education). *The Foxfire Book of Appalachian Cookery.* Dutton, 1984.

Press, Skip. *The Importance of Mark Twain.* Lucent Books, 1994.

Scott, Arthur L. *Mark Twain, Selected Criticism.* Mustang Books, 1967.

Sloane, David E.E. *Adventures of Huckleberry Finn: American Comic Vision.* Twayne Publishers, 1988.

Answer Key

Page 14

1. Huck and Tom each received 6,000 dollars in gold for finding money that robbers hid in a cave.

2. Huck says if he tells the secrets of the gang the other boys can kill Miss Watson.

3. Jim tells Huck that his father is fighting with his good and evil sides about what he should do. Huck will have much joy and sorrow in his life. He will marry twice—first time a poor girl, and then a rich one. Huck should stay away from the water.

4. Pap does not want Huck to be more educated or more civilized than he is. Unlike most parents, Pap does not want more for his son.

5. Huck is able to saw his way out of the locked cabin. He kills a wild pig, spreads the blood around, and then drags a sack of rocks into the river so people will think he has been killed.

6. Jim runs away from Miss Watson when he overhears that she will sell him down the river.

7. Huck puts a dead rattlesnake in Jim's sleeping bag. The snake's mate bites Jim. Jim is very sick for four days.

8. Huck needs to know what people are thinking about Jim and himself, so he dresses like a girl and leaves the island.

9. Mrs. Loftus notices the way Huck threads a needle, throws the piece of lead, and sits in the dress. She knows he is a boy.

10. Huck finds out that men are going to search Jackson's Island for Jim, so he hurries back to the island to get Jim. They quickly leave.

Page 19

1. Accept appropriate summaries.

2. Huck and Jim travel at night and hide on the banks of the river during the day.

3. At Cairo, Huck and Jim plan to board a boat to go up the Ohio River to the North where Jim will be free.

4. Huck has been taught that a slave is someone's property. Huck feels he will be doing a terrible injustice to Miss Watson if he helps Jim escape. (Jim hopes to eventually buy or steal his wife and two children.)

5. In order to keep some men from finding Jim, Huck pretends that "his family" on the raft has smallpox.

6. Twain describes the Grangerfords as a kind and loving family whose home is cozy and full of sentimental work. Even though they seem caring, they are having a deadly feud with the Shepherdsons.

7. One line to show Huck is happy to be back on the raft is, "You feel mighty free and easy and comfortable on a raft."

8. Colonel Sherburn tells the mob that they are cowards and would not have the nerve to come alone and try to kill him. They only get their courage from each other.

9. The king and duke constantly use American slang and speak in river dialect. Their manners are not royal, and neither are the details of their stories.

10. Jim says he cannot forgive himself for hurting his daughter when he was unaware that she was deaf. He cries because he misses her so much.

Page 24

1. Accept appropriate summaries.

2. Huck is referring to the king and duke pretending to be the uncles of the Wilks girls in order to steal their gold.

3. Dr. Robinson realizes the two are frauds. He probably knows because, being a doctor, he has traveled and seen more types of people than the rest of the people of the town.

4. Huck decides to steal the money back because the Wilks girls are so kind to him. When Mary Jane unexpectedly appears, Huck is forced to leave the money in the coffin.

Answer Key *(cont.)*

5. Mary Jane is very upset when the king and duke sell the slaves, sending the mother down river and her sons up river. Mary Jane knows that this family would be separated forever.

6. Peter Wilks' body is unearthed to see what sort of tattoo was on his chest. This would determine which set of brothers was genuine.

7. When the coffin lid is raised, the gold is discovered. The person holding Huck is so excited he lets Huck go. Huck races back to Jim and the raft.

8. The king sells Jim into slavery for 40 dollars.

9. Huck is not sure whether to write Miss Watson and tell her Jim is being held or to try and free Jim himself.

10. Huck's mind says that Jim is Miss Watson's property. His heart tells him that Jim has been a great and true friend. His heart wins out, and he plans to steal Jim.

Page 27 (Mississippi River Facts)

1. Big Water
2. 3,800 km (2,375 Miles)
3. Missouri River
4. Hernando de Soto
5. Robert Cavalier
6. Itasca
7. Minneapolis and St. Paul
8. Hannibal, Missouri
9. Gateway
10. Ohio River
11. Memphis
12. Gulf of Mexico
13. New Orleans
14. Minnesota
    Iowa
    Missouri
    Kentucky
    Louisiana
    Wisconsin
    Illinois
    Arkansas
    Tennessee
    Mississippi

Page 29

1. Accept appropriate summaries.
2. Jim tells the Phelps about the Royal Nonesuch, and the town is waiting to deal with the king and duke.

3. The people of Pikesville tar and feather the king and duke. As horrible as they have been to Huck and Jim, Huck feels that the tar and feathering is horrible and says, "Human beings can be awful cruel to one another."

4. Huck simply wants to free Jim in the simplest way. Tom says it has to be an adventure and wants to make it like the stories he has read.

5. The grindstone is too heavy for the boys to move it, so they have to free Jim to help them. Once the grindstone is inside the hut, Jim is rechained to the bed. Tom says Jim's release has to be done a certain way, but it is ironic since it is really so easy to free Jim.

6. Jim is willing to give up his freedom to save Tom's life. This shows the essential goodness of the man.

7. The doctor tells Jim's captors that Jim saved Tom's life and never tried to run to freedom.

8. Jim tells Huck that the body they saw in the house floating down the river was Huck's Pap.

9. Miss Watson has died and granted Jim his freedom in her will.

10. Huck plans to take off for the western territories because people have tried to "sivilize" him in the past and he does not want it to happen again.

Page 42 (Unit Test)

Multiple Choice

1. B
2. C
3. B
4. C
5. C

Matching

Huck-D

Jim-G

Tom-E

king-A

Sophia-F

Aunt Sally-C

Miss Watson-B

Sequence

5-2-3-1-4

Riding the River

(**Note:** See page 5 for suggestions for use.)

48